Supporting a Child with Autism

A guide for
teachers and
classroom
assistants

Sharon Powell

●●●●●●●●●●●●●●●●●●●●●●●●●●●●●●

"We are all different – it is the differences that make us individual, our individuality is what makes us interesting to other people. We should celebrate individuality."

Sharon Powell

ISBN 1 904082 39 4

A complete catalogue of BILD books, journals and training materials is available from BILD, tel 01562 723010

Contents

1 What is autism?

Some people describe autism – or autistic spectrum disorder - as a triad of impairments. These are introduced below:

• Impaired skills of social interaction

Children may have difficulties in relating to others, especially in large groups when they may appear detached. Children may also have difficulty in establishing friendships.

• Difficulties in communication and the social functions of language, including body language and facial expressions.

Occasionally a child may like the sound of a particular word and use it excessively and inappropriately. Some children may also talk for long periods about one subject with little regard for the person they are talking to.

• Restricted or stereotyped behaviours. This may include interest in one particular topic or fixation on a particular object.

For example an interest in an object or subject which is unusual, eg birthdays, coloured pencils, candles or unusual words. Sometimes children may have to perform a task in a certain order or manner, such as taking their coat off or placing their lunch box in a drawer before entering the classroom.

It is important to remember that all children are individuals. You may be supporting a child who has autistic spectrum disorder and behaves in unusual ways and presents you with many new issues. The next child you meet who is on the spectrum will be completely different and you will have new challenges to meet. Never assume that one child with autism is the same as all the others.

With patience, care, supporting the child and working with their family or carers it will be possible to get to know each child you meet as an individual and to help them to learn and make the most of the opportunities which you can offer them.

2 Your observations

You may have noticed that the child you are supporting has difficulties with the following:
• Maintaining appropriate eye contact
• Working within groups or understanding that group instructions relate to them

• Speaking at inappropriate times, not obeying the 'social rules'.

• Concentration - often children with autistic spectrum disorders are easily distracted.

• They may appear angry or upset for no apparent reason, often due to difficulties in communication or understanding their environment.

• The child with autism can sometimes feel stressed in certain situations, unfamiliar environments or when routine changes.

• Understanding similes and metaphors. It is common for the child to interpret language literally.

Don't worry if you've noticed something, which is not listed above - the child you are supporting is an individual.

3 What can I do to help?

It can be helpful to understand the child's view of the world:

• How do they make sense of their immediate environment?

Observe how the individual child makes sense of their immediate environment, and use what you have observed to support the child. For example do they like a particular colour or sound? If so, how might you use this to enable them to enjoy activities or lessons more, or reward them?

• What are the main things that stress them?

If you have identified key stressors or a trigger that may cause the child upset, where possible remove the stressor or trigger. It may be an everyday activity such as queuing for lunch. In this case, it may be possible to support the child to learn to queue without becoming stressed. You can do this by breaking the task into manageable chunks by moving them down the queue from the front a person at a time over a given period.

• What are the important routines in their life?

Some children will have routines or 'ritualistic behaviours'. It can be very difficult for the children to stop these behaviours; occasionally these behaviours can appear 'odd' or socially inappropriate. It may be necessary to support the child to enable them to behave in a socially valid or appropriate manner. Some children enjoy sensory activities. Stroking hair is an example of this - people who know a child may find this behaviour acceptable, however the casual bystander in the local shop, who finds a child who they don't know touching them in such an intimate manner may not be so accepting.

• Children who are on the autistic spectrum will often rely only on one or two senses to help them understand their environment.

Some children may rely heavily on just one or two of their senses to interpret their world. If you can identify how the child makes sense of their world it may enable you to use more appropriate strategies. Perhaps the young person you are supporting uses their sense of touch a great deal. If so, use tactile materials to encourage them to participate in activities or use water, sand or play dough.

• Identify their interest and use this to 'link to their world.'

Many children with autistic spectrum disorder have particular interests or 'fixations' on unusual subjects or objects, which they enjoy often to the exclusion of all other subjects. This may enable you to work effectively with the individual child by offering access to the interest as a reward or at specific times of the day, perhaps after lunch or play time. It will also be important to be aware of the interest and the impact it may have on the child's life, particularly if the interest may present risk to them or others. It is important to encourage a balance in the child's life - remember, denying access to an interest may increase the stress levels of the child.

4 Strategies which may help

1. A personal timetable, for very young children a pictorial or colour co-ordinated timetable, may be of particular help. Digital photographs can be helpful.

2. Help the children to focus their attention. Many children with autistic spectrum disorder like rules; these can be used to enable them to focus on particular tasks. It may be necessary to repeat the rules or if possible give the child a copy of the 'rules' to keep.

3. Teaching the concept of 'finished' enables the child to understand when an activity is finished. Establishing routines or using a red, amber and green system can help with this abstract concept.

4. Ensure that there is a consistent approach to individual children that avoids ambiguity.

5. Use a child's name to focus them especially when group instructions are given.

6. It is important to talk in clear, even and literal terms. It is unlikely the child will understand instructions if they are complex or distorted by tone. For example avoid using phrases like 'you'll be the death of me' or 'I'll send you to Coventry'.

7. Changes in routine can be extremely difficult for the child to understand and they will need to be planned carefully and explained in advance. Giving a new set of rules, 'for one day only' or offering sequenced photos to explain a change in routine may help.

8. Once the child has learnt a new skill they may not automatically transfer this to different environments, so always practice new skills in different places. For example, a kitchen will always have green cupboards and an eye level oven if that is the one that you have used most often.

9. The child may not be able to make sense of abstract concepts and these will need to be introduced carefully and with particular thought for the individual child and how they relate to abstract ideas. If you ask a child to draw a shop you may have to state exactly which one, for example there are supermarkets, corner shops, flower shops, newspaper shops... which sort of shop do you mean? Equally there are small dogs, large dogs, gran's dog, my neighbour's dog. If you want a description of a dog you will need to be fairly specific.

● ●

10. Humour and irony are not often appreciated by the child who has autistic spectrum disorder, due to the literal interpretation of language. It is best to avoid the use of irony where possible, for example 'watch the ice' may appear to be very good advice on a particularly cold day. It is possible that the child with autistic spectrum disorder may spend all play time watching the ice.

5 Quick guide to key strategies

• Use visual cues to give information - show a picture to help explain a task.

• Get the child's attention, especially when giving group instructions

• Use clear unambiguous language. Give the child time when passing on instructions and check they have understood

• Try to prevent the child from dropping their interest into every conversation or topic, especially when it is inappropriate to do so. Offer opportunities to pursue their interest at appropriate times or make it part of the routine.

• Talk to the child's parents/carers and establish continuity and ensure you are supporting strategies which are being used at home. Some children may be on special diets because their parents believe it is helpful. It would be important for you to know about this and understand which foods should be avoided.

6 When you're not sure what to do

The child I'm supporting becomes upset for no apparent reason. What can I do?

It is likely there is a cause for a child becoming upset but it may not be immediately apparent. Try to make careful notes of the behaviours you see, discuss this with colleagues, the parents or carers and work as a team to support the child.

A child in our school spends all play time in the corner of the playground, and she never seems to play with the other children.

• •

She is probably very happy; she may enjoy watching other children and find social relationships too complex or stressful. It may be possible to introduce simple playground games such as farmers in the den which include her without singling her out. She is perhaps expressing her individuality.

The little boy I work with seems to be always bumping into things.

Some children on the autistic spectrum do appear to be slightly more 'clumsy' than their peers. Support them in PE and sports activities, and always be encouraging.

We have a child who attends our school who is very naughty; he refuses to use the term Miss, Mrs or Mr to address teachers.

This is due to the fact that children very often interpret social rules literally and may not appreciate why this term is an important form of respect within school - in fact it appears to serve no purpose to them. Using such terminology is often outside the experience of most pre-school children and may need to be introduced and explained.

The same child also sticks sharp objects down his nail beds and it can cause bleeding.

This may indicate that the child is slightly stressed or is seeking stimulation. You will need to observe this behaviour carefully, discuss it with the parents and decide on an appropriate strategy. You may also need to ask for support from the school's educational psychologist.

You need not believe you must solve all problems alone, the teacher, LSW and SENCo should always work as a team, support the child, decide on appropriate strategies and support each other. There are always specialists outside your immediate environment who can offer support such as the school nurse, educational psychologist or specialist educational support team.

Supporting a child with autistic spectrum disorder can be rewarding and interesting. It can also be frustrating at times, especially when you can't understand the way in which they are behaving or why they are behaving in a particular manner.

Remember to:

• Stay positive, acknowledge your own achievements.

• Acknowledge the child's achievements, no matter how

small. It is often the small achievements that are important to the child and their parents.

• Work in co-operation with others - you do not exist in a vacuum!

• Keep a sense of humour at all times.

I have learnt to view the world in an interesting way by supporting people with autistic spectrum disorder. It has enabled me to view the world and its complexities and the many activities I take for granted in a completely different way.

• •

7 More information

Books and resources

Aarons M, Gittens T
Autism: a social skills approach for children and adolescents
Winslow Press, Bicester, 1999, ISBN 0 86388 202 1

Aarons M, Gittens T
Handbook of autism. A guide for parents and professionals
Routledge, London, 1999, ISBN 0415 16034 0

Cumine V
Autism in the early years: a practical guide
David Fulton Publishers, London, 1999, ISBN 1 85346 599 2

Dickinson P, Hannah L
It can get better – a guide for parents and carers
National Autistic Society, London, 1998, ISBN 1 899280 03 0

Howlin P
Children with autism: a guide for practitioners and carers
John Wiley Ltd, Chichester, 1998, ISBN 0471 98327 6

Jordan R, Jones G
Meeting the needs of children with autistic spectrum disorders
David Fulton Publishers, London, 1999, ISBN 1 85346 582 8

● ●

Powell S
Helping children with autism to learn
David Fulton Publishers, London, 2000, ISBN 1 85346 637 9

Contacts and Networks

Autism Cymru
6 Great Darkgate Street
Aberystwth
Ceridigion
SY23 1DE
Tel: 01970 626256

autism.west midlands
18 Highfield Road
Edgbaston
Birmingham B15 3DU
Tel: 0121 450 7580
Fax: 0121 450 7581
www.autismwestmidlands.org.uk

British Institute of Learning Disabilities (BILD)
Campion House
Green Street
Kidderminster
Worcestershire DY10 1JL
Tel: 01562 723010

Fax: 01562 723029
www.bild.org.uk

National Autistic Society
393 City Road
London EC1V 1NE
Tel: 020 7833 2299
Fax: 020 7833 9666

Scottish Society for Autistic Children
Hilton House
Alloa Business Park
Whins Road
Alloa
FK10 3SA
Tel: 01259 720044
Fax: 01259 720051